PENGUIN MODERN POETS 5

D 78

Christopher Edwards

Penguin Modern Poets

5

GREGORY CORSO
LAWRENCE FERLINGHETTI
ALLEN GINSBERG

Penguin Books

Penguin Books Ltd, Harmondsworth, Middlesex, England
Penguin Books Australia Ltd, Ringwood, Victoria, Australia

—

This selection first published 1963
Reprinted 1966, 1968

—

Copyright © Penguin Books Ltd, 1963

—

Made and printed in Great Britain
by Cox & Wyman Ltd,
London, Fakenham and Reading
Set in Monotype Garamond

Cover by Roger Mayne

Contents

ALLEN GINSBERG

ACKNOWLEDGEMENTS

The poems in this selection are taken from the following books, to whose publishers acknowledgement is made: *Gasoline* (1958), published by City Lights Books, *The Happy Birthday of Death* (1960) and *Long Live Man* (1962), published by New Directions, and *Selected Poems* (1962), published by Eyre & Spottiswoode, all by Gregory Corso; *A Coney Island of Mind* (1958), published by New Directions and Hutchinson, and *Starting from San Francisco* (1961), published by New Directions, by Lawrence Ferlinghetti; *Howl* (1956) and *Kaddish* (1961), published by City Lights Books, by Allen Ginsberg.

A collective acknowledgement is due to Ferlinghetti and City Lights Books for magazine or broadsheet publication of many of these poems.

GREGORY CORSO

The Mad Yak

I am watching them churn the last milk
    they'll ever get from me.
They are waiting for me to die;
They want to make buttons out of my bones.
Where are my sisters and brothers?
That tall monk there, loading my uncle,
    he has a new cap.
And that idiot student of his –
    I never saw that muffler before.
Poor uncle, he lets them load him.
How sad he is, how tired!
I wonder what they'll do with his bones?
And that beautiful tail!
How many shoelaces will they make of that!

In the Fleeting Hand of Time

On the steps of the bright madhouse
I hear the bearded bell shaking down the woodlawn
the final knell of my world
I climb and enter a fiery gathering of knights
they unaware of my presence lay forth sheepskin plans
and with mailcoated fingers trace my arrival
back back back when on the black steps
of Nero lyre Rome I stood
in my arms the wailing philosopher
the final call of mad history
Now my presence is known
my arrival marked by illuminated stains
The great windows of Paradise open
Down to radiant dust fall the curtains of Past Time
In fly flocks of multicoloured birds
Light winged light O the wonder of light
Time takes me by the hand
born March 26 1930 I am led 100 mph
o'er the vast market of choice
what to choose? what to choose?
Oh ———— and I leave my orange room of myth
no chance to lock away my toys of Zeus
I choose the room of Bleecker Street
A baby mother stuffs my mouth with a pale Milanese breast
I suck I struggle I cry O Olympian mother
unfamiliar this breast to me
Snows
Decade of icy asphalt doomed horses
Weak dreams Dark corridors of P.S.42 Roofs Ratthroated
    pigeons

Led 100 mph over these all too real Mafia streets
profanely I shed my Hermean wings
O Time be merciful
throw me beneath your humanity of cars
feed me to giant grey skyscrapers
exhaust my heart to your bridges
I discard my lyre of Orphic futility

And for such betrayal I climb these bright mad steps
and enter this room of paradiscal light
ephemeral
Time
a long long dog having chased its orbited tail
comes grab my hand
and leads me into conditional life

Seaspin

To drown to be slow hair
To be fish minstrelry
One eye to flick and stare
The fathomed wreck to see –
Forever down to drown
Descend the squid's conclave
Black roof the whale's belly
Oyster floor the grave –

My sea-ghost rise
And slower hair
Silverstreaks my eyes
Up up I whirl
And wonder where –

To breathe in Neptune's cup
Nudge gale and tempest
Feel the mermaid up
To stay to pin my hair
On the sea-horse's stirrup –

Marriage

Should I get married? Should I be good?
Astound the girl next door
with my velvet suit and faustus hood?
Don't take her to movies but to cemeteries
tell all about werewolf bathtubs and forked clarinets
then desire her and kiss her and all the preliminaries
and she going just so far and I understanding why
not getting angry saying You must feel! It's beautiful to
    feel!
Instead take her in my arms
lean against an old crooked tombstone
and woo her the entire night the constellations in the sky –

When she introduces me to her parents
back straightened, hair finally combed, strangled by a tie,
should I sit knees together on their 3rd degree sofa
and not ask Where's the bathroom?
How else to feel other than I am,
often thinking Flash Gordon soap –
O how terrible it must be for a young man
seated before a family and the family thinking
We never saw him before! He wants our Mary Lou!
After tea and homemade cookies they ask
What do you do for a living?
Should I tell them? Would they like me then?
Say All right get married, we're not losing a daughter
we're gaining a son –
And should I then ask Where's the bathroom?

O God, and the wedding! All her family and her friends
and only a handful of mine all scroungy and bearded
just waiting to get at the drinks and food –

And the priest! he looking at me as if I masturbated
asking me Do you take this woman
for your lawful wedded wife!
And I trembling what to say say Pie Glue!
I kiss the bride all those corny men slapping me on the back
She's all yours, boy! Ha-ha-ha!
And in their eyes you could see
some obscene honeymoon going on –
Then all that absurd rice and clanky cans and shoes
Niagara Falls! Hordes of us!
Husbands! Wives! Flowers! Chocolates!
All streaming into cosy hotels
All going to do the same thing tonight
The indifferent clerk he knowing what was going to
    happen
The lobby zombies they knowing what
The whistling elevator man he knowing
The winking bellboy knowing
Everybody knowing!
I'd be almost inclined not to do anything!
Stay up all night! Stare that hotel clerk in the eye!
Screaming: I deny honeymoon! I deny honeymoon!
running rampant into those almost climactic suites
yelling Radio belly! Cat shovel!
O I'd live in Niagara forever! in a dark cave beneath the
    Falls
I'd sit there the Mad Honeymooner
devising ways to break marriages, a scourge of bigamy
a saint of divorce –

But I should get married I should be good
How nice it'd be to come home to her
and sit by the fireplace and she in the kitchen
aproned young and lovely wanting my baby

and so happy about me she burns the roast beef
and comes crying to me and I get up from my big papa
    chair
saying Christmas teeth! Radiant brains! Apple deaf!
God what a husband I'd make! Yes, I should get married!
So much to do! like sneaking into Mr Jones' house late at
    night
and cover his golf clubs with 1920 Norwegian books
Like hanging a picture of Rimbaud on the lawnmower
Like pasting Tannu Tuva postage stamps
all over the picket fence
Like when Mrs Kindhead comes to collect
for the Community Chest
grab her and tell her There are unfavourable omens in the
    sky!
And when the mayor comes to get my vote tell him
When are you going to stop people killing whales!
And when the milkman comes leave him a note in the bottle
Penguin dust, bring me penguin dust, I want penguin
    dust –

Yet if I should get married and it's Connecticut and snow
and she gives birth to a child and I am sleepless, worn,
up for nights, head bowed against a quiet window
the past behind me,
finding myself in the most common of situations
a trembling man knowledged with responsibility
not twig-smear nor Roman coin soup –
O what would that be like!
Surely I'd give it for a nipple a rubber Tacitus
For a rattle a bag of broken Bach records
Tack Della Francesca all over its crib
Sew the Greek alphabet on its bib
And build for its playpen a roofless Parthenon

No, I doubt I'd be that kind of father
not rural not snow no quiet window
but hot smelly tight New York City
seven flights up, roaches and rats in the walls
a fat Reichian wife screeching over potatoes Get a job!
And five nose running brats in love with Batman
And the neighbours all toothless and dry haired
like those hag masses of the eighteenth century
all wanting to come in and watch TV
The landlord wants his rent
Grocery store Blue Cross Gas & Electric Knights of
  Columbus
Impossible to lie back and dream
Telephone snow, ghost parking –
No! I should not get married I should never get married!
But – imagine if I were married
to a beautiful sophisticated woman
tall and pale wearing an elegant black dress
and long black gloves
holding a cigarette holder in one hand
and a highball in the other
and we lived high up in a penthouse with a huge window
from which we could see all of New York
and even farther on clearer days
No, can't imagine myself married to that pleasant prison
  dream –

O but what about love? I forget love
not that I am incapable of love
it's just that I see love as odd as wearing shoes –
I never wanted to marry a girl who was like my mother
And Ingrid Bergman was always impossible
And there's maybe a girl now but she's already married
And I don't like men and –

but there's got to be somebody!
Because what if I'm 60 years old and not married,
all alone in a furnished room with pee stains on my under-
    wear
and everybody else is married!
All the universe married but me!

Ah, yet well I know that were a woman possible as I am
    possible
then marriage would be possible –
Like SHE in her lonely alien gaud waiting her Egyptian
    lover
so I wait – bereft of 2,000 years and the bath of life.

Written in Nostalgia for Paris

How lovely that childgirl was!
The street was wild with raiders
    but France protected their youth.
I ran to buy her a flower but a rioter
    needed blood for the FLN;
    St Michel sold the flowers
    but it was cut off by
    the Garde républicaine.
I ran up Notre Dame and called to an eagle
    that I might glide its eyes
    upon the childgirl's whereabouts,
    and did! Wings to my eyes
    I sightsailed down the sad Seine
    and saw her mightily stand
    against the fish-hooks of the fishermen.
Angel of fish! I called! It was she the child!
The harp of carp, the flute of fluke,
    the brass of bass
    the kettle of turtle
    the violin of marlin
    the tuba of barracuda
    hail whale!
That I have followed beauty – reward to know
    there's God for fish
I echo the prayers of all seas.

On the Acropolis

Temporal on the Acropolis I sat
Amid Time's slow but sure stonepecker,
Hearing pierced October cry ace old
While the Four Winds yellraked
Flakes of petrified snow.

I'd the sight of ecru-shredded Nike
Coiled in full fossilry
– Her breathing gown, her ever-loose sandal.
I'd the haycocking sunset;
Earth's texture spreading away,
And the Caryatids stood in air
Pedimenting the sky,
And about them aurora and amber,
Like silken clarions, grappled for dominancy.

How endowed with dream-love
Was I on thee, O high city!
Proud, heartfelt, boastful that I,
Exactly a youthtime,
Knew to set the table of Zeus –
The cloth, the silverware, the food thereon,
All were laid out on a small steel table
In a small cell.
And now on your great expanse with age I sat
Thanking Bullfinch and Will Durant
Their Athena and Seated Demeter;
Thanking all dream-giving
For not making Olympus a place
Where youth but serves
And in age, feasts not.

The night was right!
All the plugs of heaven seemed in!
The night was black and white –
And the moon, like a woman's breast,
Nippled the Parthenon full.
Quickly I moved in and out the pillars
Like a festering ghost straight onward entwining,
A happy Sambo tiger, a magnet heaven held –
Breathless, I stood, moon-columned,
And heard a Sophoclean lament below.
The theatre was lit! And the chorus hummed forth –
Phantoms! Phantoms in two grey ranks
Swaying back and forth, then running up!
As if to snatch and flee; then nimbling back,
Mumbling and croak-syllabling an old old woe
–All this from new lungs in a pit below.
Pressed face against a pillar I cried
Cried for my shadow that dear faithful sentry
Splashed across the world's loveliest floor.

One Day

One day while Peter-Panning the sky
I saw a man,
a man dying over the Eastern Gulph,
and I said to this man:
– The light that makes us a friend of eagles
    has made our poor wounds an interval of clouds,
    slow and creeping, calm and sad,
    in this skyful dungeon of things. –
And he replied:
– The sky is awful! The sky undarkens!
    Hermes, his wingèd foot, rests old in China!
    Rests uncontested while cloudbuds burst
    and windleaves fall!
    While my tired hands hold back
    the violent skirt of night!
    While my moss-covered feet crush
    the seaports of day! –
I left the dying man, and he must always die,
for Solitude refuses to lower a gentle hand
                upon his long sad face.

Man About to Enter Sea

Walking into the summer cold sea
arms folded
trying to keep the wave and frolicy bather
splashings from further chilling him
He moves as if not to – but I know
he'll eventually go with a NOW IN! and
become warm –

That curious warm is all too familiar
as when frogs from fish kicked
and fins winged flew
and whatever it was decided lungs
and a chance in the change above the sea –

There he wades millions of years that are legs
back into that biggest and strangest of wombs
He stands – the sea is up to his belly button
– He would it nothing more than a holiday's dip

But I feel he's algae for skin
He who calls the dinosaur his unfortunate brother
And what with crawling anthropods
oh they're only bathers on a summer shore
yet it is possible to drown in a surface of air
deem the entire earth one NOW IN! and once in
fated out again –

God? She's Black

Gases & liquids Her nature
spewing stars like eggs
from Her All Central Womb

Solids & solutions Her procedure
setting solar systems like babies
on Her All Genetic Knee

Formulae & equations Her law
punishing evolution like bad boys
by the slap of Her All Void Hand

Metals & alloys Her chore
raising telescopes like puberty
towards Her All Encompassed Eye

Sound & Light Her store
giving speed like youth
thus all Her Sons leave home

Nuclear & space Their war
creating rockets like dead men
– ever to reach Her again?

Man

Prologue to what was to be a long poem

The good scope of him is history, old and ironic;
Not modern history, unfulfilled and blurred –
Bleak damp fierce thunderous lightning days;
Poor caveman, so scared of the outside,
So afeared of its power and beauty,
Created a limit, and called that limit God –
Cell, fish, apeman, Adam;
How was the first man born?
And why has he ceased being born that way?

Air his fuel, will his engine, legs his wheels,
Eyes the steer, ears the alert;
He could not fly, but now he does –
The nails hair teeth bones blood
All in communion with the flesh;
The heart that feels all things in life
And lastly feels in death;
The hands in looks and action are masterful;
The eyes the eyes;
The penis is a magic wand,
The womb greater than Spring –

I do not know if he be Adam's heir
Or kin to ape,
No man knows; what a good driving mystery –
I can imagine a soul, the soul leaving the body,
The body feeding death, death simply a hygiene;
I can wonder the world the factory of the soul,
The soul putting on a body like a workman's coveralls,
Building, unbuilding, rebuilding.
That man can *think* soul is a great strange wonderful thing –

In the beginning was the word; man has spoken –
The Jews, the Greeks; chaos groping behind;
Exalted dignity sings; the blind angel's cithara
'Twanged no chain-reaction that World War be the Trojan
  War,
Not with the goddess Eris denied a wedding seat;
No praise of man in my war, wars have lost their legend-
  ariness –
The Bible sings man in all his glory;
Great Jew, man is hard stem of you,
Was you first spoke love, O noble survivor;
The Greeks are gone, the Egyptians have all but vanished;
Your testament yet holds –

The fall of man stands a lie before Beethoven,
A truth before Hitler –
Man is the victory of life,
And Christ be the victory of man –
King of the universe is man, creator of gods;
He knows no thing other than himself
And he knows himself the best he can;
He exists as a being of nature
And sustains all things in being;
His dream can go beyond existence –
Greater the rose?
The simple bee does not think so;
When man sings birds humble into piety;
What history can the whale empire sing?
What genius ant dare break from anthood
As can man from manhood?
King Agamemnon! Mortal man!
Ah, immortality –

Reflection in a Green Arena

Where marble stood and fell
into an eternal landscape
I stand ephemeral

Anchored to a long season in a quick life
I am not wearied
nor feel the absence of former things
my relation to my country
the weak dreams   their weaker success
the reactions to death
and lovelessness

And oh and now I know
having had enough of her
how women suffer
And that hate which men bash against men
suffers less and is with end
but a woman's loss   endless
How I wish she were yet again
with all her solemnities

Ah good consoling Greece
She was not the love I know
Having crossed over into her world
I became the sad unlove
which separates us so

Poor America poor Russia
Thank God the moon has happened them
And France Algeria what sad geo-woe
Burnt peace as obstinate as nature
seems to be the ardor of history

I wipe the dead spider
off the statue's lips
Something there is is forgotten
and what's remembered slips
Butterfly and fly and other insectai
wait themselves to die

And so it's Spring again   so what
The leaves are leaves again   no tree forgot

Friend

Friends be kept
Friends be gained
And even friends lost be friends regained
He had no foes he made them all into *friends*
A friend will die for you
Acquaintances can never make friends
Some friends want to be everybody's friend
There are friends who take you away from friends
Friends believe in friendship with a vengeance!
Some friends always want to do you favors
Some always want to get NEAR you
You can't do this to me I'm your FRIEND
My friends said FDR
Let's be friends says the USSR
Old Scrooge knew a joy in a friendless Christmas
Leopold and Loeb planning in the night!
Et tu Brute
I have many friends yet sometimes I am nobody's friend
The majority of friends are male
Girls always prefer male friends
Friends know when you're troubled
It's what they crave for!
The bonds of friendship are not inseparable
Those who haven't any friends and want some are often
　creepy
Those who have friends and don't want them are doomed
Those who haven't any friends and don't want any are grand
Those who have friends and want them seem sadly human
Sometimes I scream Friends are bondage! A madness!
All a waste of INDIVIDUAL *time* –
Without friends life would be different not miserable
Does one need a friend in heaven –

A Difference of Zoos

I went to the Hotel Broog;
and it was there I imagined myself singing *Ave Maria*
    to a bunch of hoary ligneous Brownies.
I believe in gnomes, in midges;
I believe to convert the bogeyman,
take Medusa to Kenneth's;
beg Zeus Polyphemus a new eye;
and I thanked all the men who ever lived,
thanked life the world
    for the chimera, the gargoyle,
    the sphinx, the griffin
    Rumpelstiltskin –
I sang *Ave Maria*
    for the Heap, for Groot,
    for the mugwump, for Thoth,
    the centaur, Pan;
I summoned them all to my room in the Broog,
the werewolf, the vampire, Frankenstein,
every monster imaginable
and sang and sang *Ave Maria* –
The room got to be unbearable!
I went to the zoo
and oh thank God the simple elephant.

Ares Comes and Goes

Beside me, in all its martial pose,
    walks real opportunity.
Behind me the rose is all dried up,
and my beautiful loved one intoxicated.
I'm gonna follow my new friend to the end.

The snow falls ephemeral white;
we grey it, slush it;
we're off to render the world.
Join us, human promise.

Poor world, neglect as any star.
Whether a great collision is imminent
    or not
there's no going among pyramids to grieve

Inherit of mankind
    we keep by candlelight;
something there is
    does not hold the world this night.
It's up to us;
    grass dies every step we take;
death's optimistic,
and yet it does imbibe us drive on.

He'd me carry his sword and shield;
I'd his helmet too,
but he says no
    says my posture's an embarrassment,
and takes back his weaponage to boot,
what a friend! I tell him so;
he doesn't care.

A thin ribsome horse appears;
he gets on it and . . . zoom!
    disappears.

Writ on the Steps of Puerto Rican Harlem

There's a truth limits man
A truth prevents his going any farther
The world is changing
The world *knows* it's changing
Heavy is the sorrow of the day
The old have the look of doom
The young mistake their fate in that look
This is truth
But it isn't *all* truth

Life has meaning
And I do not know the meaning
Even when I felt it were meaningless
I hoped and prayed and sought a meaning
It wasn't all frolic poesy
There were dues to pay
Summoning Death and God
I'd a wild dare to tackle Them
Death proved meaningless without Life
Yes the world is changing
But Death remains the same
It takes man away from Life
The only meaning he knows
And usually it is a sad business
This Death

I'd an innocence I'd a seriousness
I'd a humour save me from amateur philosophy
I am able to contradict my beliefs
I am able able
Because I want to know the meaning of everything
Yet sit I like a brokenness

Moaning: Oh what responsibility
I put on thee Gregory
Death and God
Hard hard it's hard

I learned life were no dream
I learned truth deceived
Man is not God
Life is a century
Death an instant

Writ in Horace Greeley Square

I know I'm one who
    even if he does see the light
still won't be completely all right
    and good for that

Yesterday I believed in man today I don't
    and tomorrow
    tomorrow's a toss-up

Somedays I see all people
    in deep pain with life
And other days
    I see them victors
living things great as to question their living

To see back and forth like that and not go crazy
    is something
Something Miss Brody ran home to jump out of
Contradiction, that good virtue,
    could prevent many a silly death

Or was it a hilarious death
the prodigal son arrives home
    'Hello pa'
    and jumps out the window

Out the window
Oh out the window is an image of man disrupts
    the image I would of him
A block away is that high diveboard
How many drove from there?
I clearly recall a huge ape dropping down

And you, Mr Greeley, what say you
    in all your bronze watchings?
What newspaper now?
Tells it man is in deep pain with life?
Man is the victory of life?

Second Night in N.Y.C. after 3 Years

I was happy I was bubbly drunk
The street was dark
I waved to a young policeman
He smiled
I went up to him and like a flood of gold
Told him all about my prison youth
About how noble and great some convicts were
And about how I just returned from Europe
Which wasn't half as enlightening as prison
And he listened attentively I told no lie
Everything was truth and humor
He laughed
He laughed
And it made me so happy I said:
'Absolve it all, kiss me!'
'No no no no!' he said
    and hurried away.

Writ on the Eve of My 32nd Birthday

A slow thoughtful spontaneous poem

I am 32 years old
and finally I look my age, if not more.
Is it a good face what's no more a boy's face?
It seems fatter. And my hair,
it's stopped being curly. Is my nose big?
The lips are the same.
And the eyes, ah the eyes get better all the time.
32 and no wife, no baby; no baby hurts,
    but there's lots of time.
I don't act silly any more.
And because of it I have to hear from so-called friends:
'You've changed. You used to be so crazy so great.'
They are not comfortable with me when I'm serious.
Let them go the the Radio City Music Hall.
32; saw all of Europe, met millions of people;
    was great for some, terrible for others.
I remember my 31st year when I cried:
'To think I may have to go another 31 years!'
I don't feel that way this birthday.
I feel I want to be wise with white hair in a tall library
    in a deep chair by a fireplace.
Another year in which I stole nothing.
8 years now and haven't stole a thing!
I stopped stealing!
But I still lie at times,
and still am shameless yet ashamed when it comes
    to asking for money.
32 years old and four hard real funny sad bad wonderful
    books of poetry
– the world owes me a million dollars.

I think I had a pretty weird 32 years.
And it weren't up to me, none of it.
No choice of two roads; if there were,
     I don't doubt I'd have chosen both.
I like to think *chance* had it I play the bell.
The clue, perhaps, is in my unbashed declaration:
'I'm good example there's such a thing as called soul.'
I love poetry because it makes me love
     and presents me life.
And of all the fires that die in me,
there's one burns like the sun;
it might not make day my personal life,
     my association with people,
     or my behaviour toward society,
but it does tell me my soul has a shadow.

LAWRENCE FERLINGHETTI

In Goya's Greatest Scenes

In Goya's greatest scenes we seem to see
                              the people of the world
         exactly at the moment when
            they first attained the title of
                              'suffering humanity'
            They writhe upon the page
                        in a veritable rage
                              of adversity
         Heaped up
                  groaning with babies and bayonets
                              under cement skies
            in an abstract landscape of blasted trees
               bent statues bats' wings and beaks
                     slippery gibbets
            cadavers and carnivorous cocks
            and all the final hollering monsters
               of the
                        'imagination of disaster'
            they are so bloody real
                        it is as if they really still existed

And they do

      Only the landscape is changed

They still are ranged along the roads
            plagued by legionaires
                        false windmills and demented roosters

They are the same people
            only further from home

on freeways fifty lanes wide
                on a concrete continent
                        spaced with bland billboards
            illustrating imbecile illusions of happiness

    The scene shows fewer tumbrils
                    but more maimed citizens
                                in painted cars
        and they have strange licence plates
        and engines
                    that devour America

Sometime during Eternity

Sometime during eternity
some guys show up
and one of them
who shows up real late
is a kind of carpenter
from some square-type place
like Galilee
and he starts wailing
and claiming he is hip
to who made heaven
and earth
and that the cat
who really laid it on us
is his Dad

And moreover
he adds
It's all writ down
on some scroll-type parchments
which some henchmen
leave lying around the Dead Sea somewheres
a long time ago
and which you won't even find
for a coupla thousand years or so
or at least for
nineteen hundred and fortyseven
of them
to be exact
and even then
nobody really believes them
or me
for that matter

You're hot
             they tell him

And they cool him

They stretch him on the Tree to cool

             And everybody after that
                                  is always making models
                     of this Tree
                          with Him hung up
and always crooning His name
                              and calling Him to come down
                 and sit in
                          on their combo
            as if he is *the* king cat
                                 who's got to blow
          or they can't quite make it

          Only he don't come down
                              from His Tree

Him just hang there
              on His Tree
                              looking real Petered out
                   and real cool
                              and also
            according to a roundup
                              of late world news
        from the usual unreliable sources
                              real dead

Dove sta amore

Dove sta amore
Where lies love
Dove sta amore
Here lies love
The ring dove love
In lyrical delight
Hear love's hillsong
Love's true willsong
Love's low plainsong
Too sweet painsong
In passages of night
Dove sta amore
Here lies love
The ring dove love
Dove sta amore
Here lies love

Autobiography

I am leading a quiet life
in Mike's Place every day
watching the champs
of the Dante Billiard Parlor
and the French pinball addicts.
I am leading a quiet life
on lower East Broadway.
I am an American.
I was an American boy.
I read the *American Boy Magazine*
and became a boy scout
in the suburbs.
I thought I was Tom Sawyer
catching crayfish in the Bronx River
and imagining the Mississippi.
I had a baseball mit
and an American Flyer bike.
I delivered the *Woman's Home Companion*
at five in the afternoon
or the *Herald Trib*
at five in the morning.
I still can hear the paper thump
on lost porches.
I had an unhappy childhood.
I saw Lindberg land.
I looked homeward
and saw no angel.
I got caught stealing pencils
from the Five and Ten Cent Store
the same month I made Eagle Scout.
I chopped trees for the C C C
and sat on them.

I landed in Normandy
in a rowboat that turned over.
I have seen the educated armies
on the beach at Dover.
I am reading *Lorna Doone*
and a life of John Most
terror of the industrialist
a bomb on his desk at all times.
I have seen the garbagemen parade
in the Columbus Day Parade
behind the glib
farting trumpeters.
I have not been out to the Cloisters
in a long time
nor to the Tuileries
but I still keep thinking
of going.
I have seen the garbagemen parade
when it was snowing.
I have eaten hotdogs in ballparks.
I have heard the Gettysburg Address
and the Ginsberg Address.
I like it here
and I won't go back
where I came from.
I too have ridden boxcars boxcars boxcars.
I have been in Asia
with Noah in the Ark.
I was in India
when Rome was built.
I have been in the Manger
with an Ass.
I have seen the Eternal Distributor
from a White Hill

in South San Franscisco
and the Laughing Woman at Loona Park
outside the Fun House
in a great rainstorm
still laughing.
I am leading a quiet life
outside of Mike's Place every day
watching the world walk by
in its curious shoes.
I once started out
to walk around the world
but ended up in Brooklyn.
That Bridge was too much for me.
I have engaged in silence
exile and cunning.
I flew too near the sun
and my wax wings fell off.
I am looking for my Old Man
whom I never knew.
I am looking for the Lost Leader
with whom I flew.
Young men should be explorers.
But Mother never told me
there'd be scenes like this.
Womb-weary
I rest
I have travelled.
I have seen goof city.
I have seen the mass mess.
I have heard Kid Ory cry.
I have heard a trombone preach.
I have heard Debussy
strained thru a sheet.
I have slept in a hundred islands

where books were trees.
I have heard the birds
that sound like bells.
I have dwelt in a hundred cities
where trees were books.
What subways what taxis what cafés!
What women with blind breasts
limbs lost among skyscrapers!
I have seen the statues of heroes
at carrefours
Danton weeping at a metro entrance
Columbus in Barcelona
pointing Westward up the Ramblas
toward the American Express
Lincoln in his stony chair
And a great Stone Face
in North Dakota.
I know that Columbus
did not invent America.
I have heard a hundred housebroken Ezra Pounds.
They should all be freed.
It is long since I was a herdsman.
I am leading a quiet life
in Mike's Place every day
reading the Classified columns.
I have read the Reader's Digest
from cover to cover
and noted the close identification
of the United States and the Promised Land
where every coin is marked
In God We Trust
but the dollar bills do not have it
being gods unto themselves.
I read the Want Ads daily

looking for a stone a leaf
an unfound door.
I hear America singing
in the Yellow Pages.
One could never tell
the soul has its rages.
I read the papers every day
and hear humanity amiss
in the sad plethora of print.
I see where Walden Pond has been drained
to make an amusement park.
I see they're making Melville
eat his whale.
I see another war is coming
but I won't be there to fight it.
I have read the writing
on the outhouse wall.
I helped Kilroy write it.
I marched up Fifth Avenue
blowing on a bugle in a tight platoon
but hurried back to the Casbah
looking for my dog.
I see a similarity
between dogs and me.
Dogs are the true observers
walking up and down the world
thru the Molloy country.
I have walked down alleys
too narrow for Chryslers.
I have seen a hundred horseless milkwagons
in a vacant lot in Astoria.
Ben Shahn never painted them
but they're there
askew in Astoria.

I have heard the junkman's obbligato.
I have ridden superhighways
and believed the billboard's promises
Crossed the Jersey Flats
and seen the Cities of the Plain
And wallowed in the wilds of Westchester
with its roving bands of natives
in stationwagons.
I have seen them.
I am the man.
I was there.
I suffered
somewhat.
I am an American.
I have a passport.
I did not suffer in public.
And I'm too young to die.
I am a selfmade man.
And I have plans for the future.
I am in line
for a top job.
I may be moving on
to Detroit.
I am only temporarily
a tie salesman.
I am a good Joe.
I am an open book
to my boss.
I am a complete mystery
to my closest friends.
I am leading a quiet life
in Mike's Place every day
contemplating my navel.
I am a part

of the body's long madness.
I have wandered in various nightwoods.
I have leaned in drunken doorways.
I have written wild stories
without punctuation.
I am the man.
I was there.
I suffered.
I sat in an uneasy chair.
I am a tear of the sun.
I am a hill
where poets run.
I invented the alphabet
after watching the flight of cranes
who made letters with their legs.
I am a lake upon a plain.
I am a word
in a tree.
I am a hill of poetry.
I am a raid
on the inarticulate.
I have dreamt
that all my teeth fell out
but my tongue lived
to tell the tale.
For I am a still
of poetry.
I am a bank of song.
I am a playerpiano
in an abandoned casino
on a seaside esplanade
in a dense fog
still playing.
I see a similarity

between the Laughing Woman
and myself.
I have heard the sound of summer
in the rain.
I have seen girls on boardwalks
have complicated sensations.
I understand their hesitations.
I am a gatherer of fruit.
I have seen how kisses
cause euphoria.
I have seen giraffes in junglegyms
their necks like love
wound around the iron circumstances
of the world.
I have seen the Venus Aphrodite
armless in her drafty corridor.
I have heard a siren sing
at One Fifth Avenue.
I have seen the White Goddess dancing
in the Rue des Beaux Arts
on the Fourteenth of July
and the Beautiful Dame Without Mercy
picking her nose in Chumley's.
She did not speak English.
She had yellow hair
and a hoarse voice
and no bird sang.
I am leading a quiet life
in Mike's Place every day
watching the pocket pool players
making the minestrone scene
wolfing the macaronis
and I have read somewhere
the Meaning of Existence

yet have forgotten
just exactly where.
But I am the man
And I'll be there
And I may cause the lips
of those who are asleep
to speak
And I may make my notebooks
into sheaves of grass
And I may write my own
eponymous epitaph
instructing the horsemen
to pass.

Euphoria

As I approach the state of pure euphoria
   I find I need a largersize typewriter case
   to carry my underwear in
   and scars on my conscience
   are wounds imbedded in
   the gum eraser of my skin
   which still erases itself
As I approach the state of pure euphoria
   moon hides hot face in cool rice rain
   of Chinese painting
   and I cannot sleep because of the thunder
   under the summer afternoon
   in which a girl puts on a record of
   crazy attempts to play a saxophone
   punctuated by terrible forced laughter
   in another room
As I approach the state of pure euphoria
   they are building all the cities now
   on only one side of the street
   and my shoes walk up sides of buildings
   leaving tracks of windows
   with their soles of panes about to crack
   and shoe-tongues of roll-up shades alack
   I see my roll-up tongue upon a string
   and see my face upon the stick of it
   as on a pendulum about to swing
   a playing-card image with bound feet
   an upside-down hanged Villon
   And Mama recedes in a hand-held photo
   and Dad is named Ludwig
   in a lost real estate project ended in water

Saratoga Avenue Yonkers
where I now hang and swing
on a last tree that stands drinking
and where I'd still sing partsongs
in a field of rapture
but an angel has me by the balls
and my castrato voice comes out too small
with a girl that puts a laughing record on
in another room
As I approach the state of pure euphoria
my eyes are gringo spies and I
may anytime be changed to birds
by a Tungus explosion that controls time
but I am no apocalyptic kid
and cannot sleep because of the thunder
under the summer afternoon
and my dumb bird's eye starts
out of my head
and flies around the world
in which a girl puts on
her record made of flesh
And I am animals without clothes
looking for a naked unity
but I'm divided up into countries
and I'm in Tibet on potato legs
and am a strange kind of clown
with befloured face and hair plastered down
and cannot sleep because of the thunder
under the needle my flesh turns under
She has turned it on
She has turned it over
She has turned me on
to play my other side

Her breasts bloom
figs burst
sun is white
I'll never come back
I wear Egyptian clothing

Big Fat Hairy Vision of Evil

I

Evil evil evil evil
World is evil
Life is evil
All is evil
if i ride the horse of hate
with its evil hooded eye
turning world to evil
Evil is death warmed over
Evil is Live spelled backward
Evil is lamb burning bright
Evil is love fried upon a spit
and turned upon itself
Evil is sty in eye of universe
hung upon a coughing horse
that follows me at night
thru a hollow street
wearing blinders
Evil is green gloves inside out
next to a double martini
on a cocktail table
Evil is lush with horse teeth
Evil is running after me
with glue feet
i'm running
Evil is screwing strangers
after cocktail parties
Poor dear flesh not evil
Lonely meat not evil
But evil is gooking
in my window

i am paranoid about evil
Evil is forty years old
and in my wrong mind
Evil is being out of my head
asleep or awake
Evil passes blind
thru filtertips of mind
in pot visions
where a horse walks
a horse who wants to eat me
Horse eats consciousness
i am afraid of it
i am running
i hate you evil
mad horse
We all go mad
when we die
but to ride mad horse alive
is a form of dying
each mad day a death
i am paranoid about it
Evil is out to catch me
Horse is humping after me
wearing blinders
Horse wants me to mount
Horse wants me to ride
without a halter
i am running from it
with two feet
i'm afraid
i don't want to die

2

Evil evil evil evil evil evil evil
even if three naked monkeys
see no hear no speak no evil
Ebony Buddha With Three Eyes
is evil to evil eyes
Bronze Image of Dancing Krishna
is evil
Tibetan Conquerer of Death
draped in human skin
is evil
Singing Bodhisattva
is evil
in evil eyes
All those broody figures
running after me
evil eyeballs
rolling after me
will catch up to me
stony flowers fall on me
if i don't watch out
Flowers aren't evil
but Power is evil
Captain Bigarini
with his sad sad salutes
is evil
Naked Lunch is evil lunch
because it is the brunch of hate
i am not ready to eat it
i am not that hungry
i am afraid
i cannot run forever
i'm a relay runner

with a hollow baton
with a screwy message in it
which I can't quite decipher
a strange message
an ecstatic message
in a hollow baton
shuttled thru the tubes of earth
A Paris pneumatique
lost in Macy's basement
i must not drop it and lose the message
which i've never been able to read
on the run
i'm still running with it
Horse still running behind
Horse will catch me in the living end
He'll lie down on top of me
in my horsehair grave
He will gnaw my lowest bone
with his dingbat teeth
He will stretch his legs along my limbs
to make me one with him
Horse will lick my horsy face
with his gluepot tongue
Horse will puke on me
Poop his baked potatoes out on me
in death's insanity
and i will eat that naked lunch
that turns me into him
in the death of that god
which is consciousness itself
Ah but i will not look out
before that date
thru Horse's fur windows
and vomit landscapes!

He

(*to Allen Ginsberg*)

He is one of the prophets come back
He is one of the wiggy prophets come back
He had a beard in the Old Testament
    but shaved it off in Paterson
He has a microphone around his neck
    at a poetry reading
    and he is more than one poet
    and he is an old man perpetually writing a poem
    about an old man
    whose every third thought is Death
    and who is writing a poem
    about an old man
    whose every third thought is Death
    and who is writing a poem
    Like the picture on a Quaker Oats box
    that shows a figure holding up a box
    upon which is a picture of a figure
    holding up a box
    and the figure smaller and smaller
    and further away each time
    a picture of shrinking reality itself
He is one of the prophets come back
    to see to hear to file a revised report
    on the present state
    of the shrinking world
He has buttonhooks in his eyes
    with which he fastens on
    to every foot of existence
    and on to every shoestring rumor
    of the nature of reality

And his eye fixes itself
on every stray person or thing
and waits for it to move
like a cat with a dead white mouse
suspecting it of hiding
some small clew to existence
and he waits gently
for it to reveal itself
or herself or himself
and he is gentle as the lamb of God
made into mad cutlets
And he picks up every suspicious object
and he picks up every person or thing
examining it and shaking it
like a white mouse with a piece of string
who thinks the thing is alive
and shakes it to speak
and shakes it alive
and shakes it to speak
He is a cat who creeps at night
and sleeps his buddhahood in the violet hour
and listens for the sound of three hands about to clap
and reads the script of his brainpan
his heiroglyph of existence
He is a talking asshole on a stick
he is a walkie-talkie on two legs
and he holds his phone to his ear
and he holds his phone to his mouth
and hears *Death death*
He has one head with one tongue hung
in the back of his mouth
and he speaks with an animal tongue
and man has devised a language

that no other animal understands
and his tongue sees and his tongue speaks
and his own ear hears what is said
and clings to his head
and hears *Death death*
and he has a tongue to say it
that no other animal understands
He is a forked root walking
with a knot-hole eye in the middle of his head
and his eye turns outward and inward
and sees and is mad
and is mad and sees
And he is the mad eye of the fourth person singular
of which nobody speaks
and he is the voice of the fourth person singular
in which nobody speaks
and which yet exists
with a long head and a foolscap face
and the long mad hair of death
of which nobody speaks
And he speaks of himself and he speaks of the dead
of his dead mother and his Aunt Rose
with their long hair and their long nails
that grow and grow
and they come back in his speech without a manicure
And he has come back with his black hair
and his black eye and his black shoes
and the big black book of his report
And he is a big black bird with one foot raised
to hear the sound of life reveal itself
on the shell of his sensorium
and he speaks to sing to get out of his skin
and he pecks with his tongue on the shell of it
and he knocks with his eye on the shell

and sees *light light* and hears *death death*
　of which nobody speaks
For he is a head with a head's vision
　and his is the lizard's look
　and his unbuttoned vision is the door
　in which he stands and waits and hears
　the hand that knocks and claps and claps and knocks
　his *Death Death*
For he is his own ecstatic illumination
　and he is his own hallucination
　and he is his own shrinker
　and his eye turns in the shrinking head of the world
　and hears his organ speak *Death Death*
　a deaf music
For he has come at the end of the world
　and he is the flippy flesh made word
　and he speaks the word he hears in his flesh
　and the word is
　　　　Death

Underwear

I didn't get much sleep last night
thinking about underwear
Have you ever stopped to consider
underwear in the abstract
When you really dig into it
some shocking problems are raised
Underwear is something
we all have to deal with
Everyone wears
some kind of underwear
Even Indians
wear underwear
Even Cubans
wear underwear
The Pope wears underwear I hope
Underwear is worn by Negroes
The Governor of Louisiana
wears underwear
I saw him on TV
He must have had tight underwear
He squirmed a lot
Underwear can really get you in a bind
Negroes often wear
white underwear
which may lead to trouble
You have seen the underwear ads
for men and women
so alike but so different
Women's underwear holds things up
Men's underwear holds things down
Underwear is one thing
men and women have in common

Underwear is all we have between us
You have seen the three-color pictures
with crotches encircled
to show the areas of extra strength
and three-way stretch
promising full freedom of action
Don't be deceived
It's all based on the two-party system
which doesn't allow much freedom of choice
the way things are set up
America in its Underwear
struggles thru the night
Underwear controls everything in the end
Take foundation garments for instance
They are really fascist forms
of underground government
making people believe
something but the truth
telling you what you can or can't do
Did you ever try to get around a girdle
Perhaps Non-Violent Action
is the only answer
Did Gandhi wear a girdle?
Did Lady Macbeth wear a girdle?
Was that why Macbeth murdered sleep?
And that spot she was always rubbing –
Was it really in her underwear?
Modern anglosaxon ladies
must have huge guilt complexes
always washing and washing and washing
Out damned spot – rub don't blot –
Underwear with spots very suspicious
Underwear with bulges very shocking
Underwear on clothesline a great flag of freedom

Someone has escaped his Underwear
May be naked somewhere
Help!
But don't worry
Everybody's still hung up in it
There won't be no real revolution
And poetry still the underwear of the soul
And underwear still covering
a multitude of faults
in the geological sense –
strange sedimentary stones, inscrutable cracks!
And that only the beginning
For does not the body stay alive
after death
and still need its underwear
or outgrow it
some organs said to reach full maturity
only after the head stops holding them back?
If I were you I'd keep aside
an oversize pair of winter underwear
Do not go naked into that good night
And in the meantime
keep calm and warm and dry
No use stirring ourselves up prematurely
'over Nothing'
Move forward with dignity
hand in vest
Don't get emotional
And death shall have no dominion
There's plenty of time my darling
Are we not still young and easy
Don't shout

Come Lie with Me and Be My Love

Come lie with me and be my love

Love lie with me

Lie down with me

Under the cypress tree

In the sweet grasses

Where the wind lieth

Where the wind dieth

As night passes

Come lie with me

All night with me

And have enough of kissing me

And have enough of making love

And let my lizard speak to thee

And let our two selves speak

All night under the cypress tree

Without making love

One Thousand Fearful Words for
Fidel Castro

I am sitting in Mike's Place trying to figure out
what's going to happen
without Fidel Castro
Among the salami sandwiches and spittoons
I see no solution
It's going to be a tragedy
I see no way out
among the admen and slumming models
and the brilliant snooping columnists
who are qualified to call Castro psychotic
because they no doubt are doctors
and have examined him personally
and know a paranoid hysterical tyrant when they see one
because they have it on first hand
from personal observation by the CIA
and the great disinterested news services
And Hearst is dead but his great Cuban wire still stands:
'You get the pictures, I'll make the War'
I see no answer
I see no way out
among the paisanos playing pool
it looks like Curtains for Fidel
They're going to fix his wagon
in the course of human events

In the back of Mike's the pinball machines
shudder and leap from the floor
when Cuban Charlie shakes them
and tries to work his will

on one named 'Independence Sweepstakes'
Each pinball wandered lonely as a man
siphons thru and sinks
no matter how he twists and turns
A billiardball falls in a felt pocket
like a peasant in a green landscape
You're whirling around in your little hole
Fidel
and you'll soon sink
in the course of human events

On the nickelodeon a cowboy ballad groans
'Got myself a Cadillac' the cowhand moans
He didn't get it in Cuba, baby
Outside in the night of North Beach America
the new North American cars flick by
from Motorama
their headlights never bright enough
to dispel this night
in the course of human events

Three creepy men come in
One is Chinese
One is Negro
One is some kind of crazy Indian
They look like they may have been
walking up and down in Cuba
but they haven't
All three have hearing aids
It's a little deaf brotherhood of Americans
The skinny one screws his hearing aid
in his skinny ear
He's also got a little transistor radio
the same size as his hearing aid box

For a moment I confuse the two
The radio squawks
some kind of memorial program:
'When in the course of human events
it becomes necessary for one people
to dissolve the political bonds
which have connected them with another –'
I see no way out
no escape
He's tuned in on your frequency, Fidel
but can't hear it
There's interference
It's going to be
a big evil tragedy
They're going to fix you, Fidel
with your big Cuban cigar
which you stole from us
and your army surplus hat
which you probably also stole
and your Beat beard

History may absolve you, Fidel
but we'll dissolve you first, Fidel
You'll be dissolved in history
We've got the solvent
we've got the chaser
and we'll have a little party
somewhere down your way, Fidel
It's going to be a Gas
As they say in Guatemala

Outside of Mike's Place now
an ambulance sirens up
It's a midnight murder or something

Some young bearded guy stretched on the sidewalk
with blood sticking out
Here's your little tragedy, Fidel
They're coming to pick you up
and stretch you on their Stretcher
That's what happens, Fidel
when in the course of human events
it becomes necessary for one people to dissolve
the bonds of International Tel & Tel
and United Fruit
Fidel
How come you don't answer anymore
Fidel
Did they cut you off our frequency
We've closed down our station anyway
We've turned you off, Fidel

I was sitting in Mike's Place, Fidel
waiting for someone else to act
like a good Liberal
I hadn't quite finished reading Camus' *Rebel*
so I couldn't quite recognize you, Fidel
walking up and down your island
when they came for you, Fidel
'My Country or Death' you told them
Well you've got your little death, Fidel
like old Honest Abe
one of your boyhood heroes
who also had his little Civil War
and was a different kind of Liberator
(since no one was shot in his war)
and also was murdered
in the course of human events

Fidel . . . Fidel . . .
your coffin passes by
thru lanes and streets you never knew
thru day and night, Fidel
While lilacs last in the dooryard bloom, Fidel
your futile trip is done
yet is not done
and is not futile
I give you my sprig of laurel

ALLEN GINSBERG

A Supermarket in California

What thoughts I have of you tonight, Walt Whitman, for I walked down the sidestreets under the trees with a headache self-conscious looking at the full moon.

In my hungry fatigue, and shopping for images, I went into the neon fruit supermarket, dreaming of your enumerations!

What peaches and what penumbras! Whole families shopping at night! Aisles full of husbands! Wives in the avocados, babies in the tomatoes! – and you, Garcia Lorca, what were you doing down by the watermelons?

I saw you, Walt Whitman, childless, lonely old grubber, poking among the meats in the refrigerator and eyeing the grocery boys.

I heard you asking questions of each: Who killed the pork chops? What price bananas? Are you my Angel?

I wandered in and out of the brilliant stacks of cans following you, and followed in my imagination by the store detective.

We strode down the open corridors together in our solitary fancy tasting artichokes, possessing every frozen delicacy, and never passing the cashier.

Where are we going, Walt Whitman? The doors close in an hour. Which way does your beard point tonight?

(I touch your book and dream of our odyssey in the supermarket and feel absurd.)

Will we walk all night through solitary streets? The trees add shade to shade, lights out in the houses, we'll both be lonely.

Will we stroll dreaming of the lost America of love past blue automobiles in driveways, home to our silent cottage?

Ah, dear father, graybeard, lonely old courage-teacher, what America did you have when Charon quit poling his ferry and you got out on a smoking bank and stood watching the boat disappear on the black waters of Lethe?

Sunflower Sutra

I walked on the banks of the tincan banana dock and sat
down under the huge shade of a Southern Pacific locomotive to look at the sunset over the box house hills
and cry.

Jack Kerouac sat beside me on a busted rusty iron pole,
companion, we thought the same thoughts of the soul,
bleak and blue and sad-eyed, surrounded by the
gnarled steel roots of trees of machinery.

The oily water on the river mirrored the red sky, sun sank
on top of final Frisco peaks, no fish in that stream, no
hermit in those mounts, just ourselves rheumy-eyed
and hungover like old bums on the riverbank, tired
and wily.

Look at the Sunflower, he said, there was a dead gray
shadow against the sky, big as a man, sitting dry on top
of a pile of ancient sawdust –

– I rushed up enchanted – it was my first sunflower,
memories of Blake – my visions – Harlem

and Hells of the Eastern rivers, bridges clanking Joes
Greasy Sandwiches, dead baby carriages, black tread-
less tires forgotten and unretreaded, the poem of the
riverbank, condoms & pots, steel knives, nothing stain-
less, only the dank muck and the razor sharp artifacts
passing into the past –

and the gray Sunflower poised against the sunset, crackly
bleak and dusty with the smut and smog and smoke of
olden locomotives in its eye –

corolla of bleary spikes pushed down and broken like a
battered crown, seeds fallen out of its face, soon-to-
be-toothless mouth of sunny air, sunrays obliterated on
its hairy head like a dried wire spiderweb,

leaves stuck out like arms out of the stem, gestures from

the sawdust root, broke pieces of plaster fallen out of
the black twigs, a dead fly in its ear,

Unholy battered old thing you were, my sunflower O my
soul, I loved you then!

The grime was no man's grime but death and human locomotives,

all that dress of dust, that veil of darkened railroad skin,
that smog of cheek, that eyelid of black mis'ry, that
sooty hand or phallus or protuberance of artificial
worse-than-dirt – industrial – modern – all that
civilization spotting your crazy golden crown –

and those blear thoughts of death and dusty loveless eyes
and ends and withered roots below, in the home-pile
of sand and sawdust, rubber dollar bills, skin of
machinery, the guts and innards of the weeping
coughing car, the empty lonely tincans with their rusty
tongues alack, what more could I name, the smoked
ashes of some cock cigar, the cunts of wheelbarrows
and the milky breasts of cars, wornout asses out of
chairs & sphincters of dynamos – all these

entangled in your mummied roots – and you there standing
before me in the sunset, all your glory in your form!

A perfect beauty of a sunflower! a perfect excellent lovely
sunflower existence! a sweet natural eye to the new hip
moon, woke up alive and excited grasping in the sunset shadow sunrise golden monthly breeze!

How many flies buzzed round you innocent of your grime,
while you cursed the heavens of the railroad and your
flower soul?

Poor dead flower? when did you forget you were a flower?
when did you look at your skin and decide you were an
impotent dirty old locomotive? the ghost of a locomotive? the specter and shade of a once powerful mad
American locomotive?

You were never no locomotive, Sunflower, you were a
sunflower!

And you Locomotive, you are a locomotive, forget me not!

So I grabbed up the skeleton thick sunflower and stuck it at
my side like a scepter,

and deliver my sermon to my soul, and Jack's soul too, and
anyone who'll listen,

- We're not our skin of grime, we're not our dread bleak
dusty imageless locomotive, we're all beautiful golden
sunflowers inside, we're blessed by our own seed &
golden hairy naked accomplishment-bodies growing
into mad black formal sunflowers in the sunset, spied
on by our eyes under the shadow of the mad locomotive riverbank sunset Frisco hilly tincan evening
sitdown vision.

America

America I've given you all and now I'm nothing.
America two dollars and twenty-seven cents January 17,
1956.
I can't stand my own mind.
America when will we end the human war?
Go fuck yourself with your atom bomb.
I don't feel good don't bother me.
I won't write my poem till I'm in my right mind.
America when will you be angelic?
When will you take off your clothes?
When will you look at yourself through the grave?
When will you be worthy of your million Trotskyites?
America why are your libraries full of tears?
America when will you send your eggs to India?
I'm sick of your insane demands.
When can I go into the supermarket and buy what I need
with my good looks?
America after all it is you and I who are perfect not the next
world.
Your machinery is too much for me.
You made me want to be a saint.
There must be some other way to settle this argument.
Burroughs is in Tangiers I don't think he'll come back it's
sinister.
Are you being sinister or is this some form of practical
joke?
I'm trying to come to the point.
I refuse to give up my obsession.
America stop pushing I know what I'm doing.
America the plum blossoms are falling.
I haven't read the newspapers for months, everyday some-
body goes on trial for murder.

America I feel sentimental about the Wobblies.
America I used to be a communist when I was a kid I'm not
    sorry.
I smoke marijuana every chance I get.
I sit in my house for days on end and stare at the roses in
    the closet.
When I go to Chinatown I get drunk and never get laid.
My mind is made up there's going to be trouble.
You should have seen me reading Marx.
My psychoanalyst thinks I'm perfectly right.
I won't say the Lord's Prayer.
I have mystical visions and cosmic vibrations.
America I still haven't told you what you did to Uncle Max
    after he came over from Russia.

I'm addressing you.
Are you going to let your emotional life be run by *Time
    Magazine*?
I'm obsessed by *Time Magazine*.
I read it every week.
Its cover stares at me every time I slink past the corner
    candystore.
I read it in the basement of the Berkeley Public Library.
It's always telling me about responsibility. Businessmen are
    serious.   Movie producers are serious. Everybody's
    serious but me.
It occurs to me that I am America.
I am talking to myself again.

Asia is rising against me.
I haven't got a chinaman's chance.
I'd better consider my national resources.
My national resources consist of two joints of marijuana

millions of genitals an unpublishable private literature that goes 1,400 miles an hour and twentyfive thousand mental institutions.

I say nothing about my prisons nor the millions of underprivileged who live in my flowerpots under the light of five hundred suns.

I have abolished the whorehouses of France, Tangiers is the next to go.

My ambition is to be President despite the fact that I'm a Catholic.

America how can I write a holy litany in your silly mood?

I will continue like Henry Ford my strophes are as individual as his automobiles more so they're all different sexes.

America I will sell you strophes $2500 apiece $500 down on your old strophe

America free Tom Mooney

America save the Spanish Loyalists

America Sacco & Vanzetti must not die

America I am the Scottsboro boys.

America when I was seven momma took me to Communist Cell meetings they sold us garbanzos a handful per ticket a ticket costs a nickel and the speeches were free everybody was angelic and sentimental about the workers it was all so sincere you have no idea what a good thing the party was in 1835 Scott Nearing was a grand old man a real mensch Mother Bloor made me cry I once saw Israel Amter plain. Everybody must have been a spy.

America you don't really want to go to war.

America it's them bad Russians.

Them Russians them Russians and them Chinamen. And them Russians.

The Russia wants to eat us alive. The Russia's power mad.
  She wants to take our cars from out our garages.

Her wants to grab Chicago. Her needs a Red Readers'
  Digest. Her wants our auto plants in Siberia. Him big
  bureaucracy running our fillingstations.

That no good. Ugh. Him make Indians learn read. Him
  need big black niggers. Hah. Her make us all work
  sixteen hours a day. Help.

America this is quite serious.

America this is the impression I get from looking in the
  television set.

America is this correct?

I'd better get right down to the job.

It's true I don't want to join the Army or turn lathes in
  precision parts factories, I'm nearsighted and psycho-
  pathic anyway.

America I'm putting my queer shoulder to the wheel.

*

* *

POEM
Rocket

'Be a Star-screwer!' – Gregory Corso

Old moon my eyes are new moon with human footprint
no longer Romeo Sadface in drunken river Loony Pierre
    eyebrow, goof moon
O possible moon in Heaven we get to first of ageless con-
    stellations of names
as God is possible as All is possible so we'll reach another
    life.

Moon politicians earth weeping and warring in eternity
tho not one star disturbed by screaming madmen from
    Hollywood
oil tycoons from Romania making secret deals with flabby
    green Plutonians –
slave camps on Saturn Cuban revolutions on Mars?
Old life and new side by side, will Catholic church find
    Christ on Jupiter
Mohammed rave in Uranus will Buddha be acceptable on
    the stolid planets
or will we find Zoroastrian temples flowering on Neptune?

What monstrous new ecclesiastical design on the entire
  universe unfolds in the dying Pope's brain?
Scientist alone is true poet he gives us the moon
he promises the stars he'll make us a new universe if it
  comes to that
O Einstein I should have sent you my flaming mss.
O Einstein I should have pilgrimaged to your white hair!

O fellow travellers I write you a poem in Amsterdam in the
  Cosmos
where Spinoza ground his magic lenses long ago
I write you a poem long ago
already my feet are washed in death
Here I am naked without identity
with no more body than the fine black tracery of pen mark
  on soft paper
as star talks to star multiple beams of sunlight all the same
  myriad thought
in one fold of the universe where Whitman was
and Blake and Shelley saw Milton dwelling as in a starry
  temple brooding in his blindness seeing all –
Now at last I can speak to you beloved brothers of an
  unknown moon
real Yous squatting in whatever form amidst Platonic
  Vapors of Eternity
I am another Star.
Will you eat my poems or read them
or gaze with aluminum blind plates on sunless pages?
do you dream or translate & accept data with indifferent
  droopings of antennae?
do I make sense to your flowery green receptor eyesockets?
  do you have visions of God?
Which way will the sunflower turn surrounded by millions
  of suns?

This is my rocket my personal rocket I send up my message
   Beyond
Someone to hear me there
My immortality
without steel or cobalt basalt or diamond gold or mercurial
   fire
without passports filing cabinets bits of paper warheads
without myself finally
pure thought
message all and everywhere the same
I send up my rocket to land on whatever planet awaits it
preferably religious sweet planets no money
fourth dimensional planets where Death shows movies
plants speak (courteously) of ancient physics and poetry
   itself is manufactured by the trees
the final Planet where the Great Brain of the Universe sits
   waiting for a poem to land in His golden pocket
joining the other notes mash-notes love-sighs complaints-
   musical shrieks of despair and the million unutterable
   thoughts of frogs
I send you my rocket of amazing chemical
more than my hair my sperm or the cells of my body
the speeding thought that flies upward with my desire as
   instantaneous as the universe and faster than light
and leave all other questions unfinished for the moment to
   turn back to sleep in my dark bed on earth.

Europe! Europe!

World world world
I sit in my room
imagine the future
sunlight falls on Paris
I am alone there is no
one whose love is perfect
man has been mad man's
love is not perfect I
have not wept enough
my breast will be heavy
till death the cities
are specters of cranks
of war the cities are
work & brick & iron &
smoke of the furnace of
selfhood makes tearless
eyes red in London but
no eye meets the sun

Flashed out of sky it
hits Lord Beaverbrook's
white modern solid
paper building leaned
in London's street to
bear last yellow beams
old ladies absently gaze
thru fog toward heaven
poor pots on windowsills
snake flowers to street
Trafalgar's fountains splash
on noon-warmed pigeons
Myself beaming in ecstatic

wilderness on St Paul's dome
seeing the light on London
or here on a bed in Paris
sunglow through the high
window on plaster walls

Meek crowd underground
saints perish creeps
streetwomen meet lacklove
under gaslamp and neon
no woman in house loves
husband in flower unity
nor boy loves boy soft
fire in breast politics
electricity scares downtown
radio screams for money
police light on TV screens
laughs at dim lamps in
empty rooms tanks crash
thru bombshell no dream
of man's joy is made movie
think factory pushes junk
autos tin dreams of Eros
mind eats its flesh in
geekish starvation and no
man's fuck is holy for
man's work is most war

Bony China hungers brain
wash over power dam and
America hides mad meat
in refrigerator Britain
cooks Jerusalem too long
France eats oil and dead

salad arms & legs in Africa
loudmouth devours Arabia
negro and white warring
against the golden nuptial
Russia manufacture feeds
millions but no drunk can
dream Mayakovsky's suicide
rainbow over machinery
and backtalk to the sun

I lie in bed in Europe
alone in old red under
wear symbolic of desire
for union with immortality
but man's love's not perfect
in February it rains
as once for Baudelaire
one hundred years ago
planes roar in the air
cars race thru streets
I know where they go
to death but that is O K
it is that death comes
before life that no man
has loved perfectly no one
gets bliss in time new
mankind is not born that
I weep for this antiquity
and herald the Millennium
for I saw the Atlantic sun
rayed down from a vast cloud
at Dover on the sea cliffs
tanker size of ant heaved
up on ocean under shining

cloud and seagull flying
thru sun light's endless
ladders streaming in Eternity
to ants in the myriad fields
of England to sun flowers
bent up to eat infinity's
minute gold dolphins leaping
thru Mediterranean rainbow
White smoke and steam in Andes
Asia's rivers glittering
blind poets deep in lone
Apollonic radiance on hillsides
littered with empty tombs

To Aunt Rose

Aunt Rose – now – might I see you
with your thin face and buck tooth smile and pain
           of rheumatism – and a long black heavy shoe
             for your bony left leg
limping down the long hall in Newark on the running carpet
           past the black grand piano
           in the day room
                where the parties were
    and I sang Spanish loyalist songs
          in a high squeaky voice
              (hysterical) the committee listening
        while you limped around the room
          collected the money –
Aunt Honey, Uncle Sam, a stranger with a cloth arm
          in his pocket
            and huge young bald head
              of Abraham Lincoln Brigade

– your long sad face
        your tears of sexual frustration
           (what smothered sobs and bony hips
              under the pillows of Osborne Terrace)
    – the time I stood on the toilet seat naked
       and you powdered my thighs with Calomine
       against the poison ivy – my tender
          and shamed first black curled hairs
what were you thinking in secret heart then
        knowing me a man already –
and I an ignorant girl of family silence on the thin pedestal
         of my legs in the bathroom – Museum of Newark.

Aunt Rose
Hitler is dead, Hitler is in Eternity; Hitler is with
Tamburlane and Emily Brontë

Though I see you walking still, a ghost on Osborne Terrace
down the long dark hall to the front door
limping a little with a pinched smile
in what must have been a silken
flower dress
welcoming my father, the Poet, on his visit to Newark
– see you arriving in the living room
dancing on your crippled leg
and clapping hands his book
had been accepted by Liveright

Hitler is dead and Liveright's gone out of business
The Attic of the Past and Everlasting Minute are out of print
Uncle Harry sold his last silk stocking
Claire quit interpretive dancing school
Buba sits a wrinkled monument in Old
Ladies Home blinking at new babies

last time I saw you was the hospital
pale skull protruding under ashen skin
blue veined unconscious girl
in an oxygen tent
the war in Spain has ended long ago
Aunt Rose

The Lion for Real

'Soyez muette pour moi, contemplative Idole . . .'

I came home and found a lion in my living room
Rushed out on the fire-escape screaming Lion! Lion!
Two stenographers pulled their brunette hair and banged
the window shut
I hurried home to Paterson and stayed two days.

Called up my old Reichian analyst
who'd kicked me out of therapy for smoking marijuana
'It's happened' I panted 'There's a Lion in my room'
'I'm afraid any discussion would have no value' he hung
up.

I went to my old boyfriend we got drunk with his girl-
friend
I kissed him and announced I had a lion with a mad
gleam in my eye
We wound up fighting on the floor I bit his eyebrow & he
kicked me out
I ended masturbating in his jeep parked in the street moaning 'Lion.'

Found Joey my novelist friend and roared at him 'Lion!'
He looked at me interested and read me his spontaneous
ignu high poetries
I listened for lions all I heard was Elephant Tiglon Hip-
pogryph Unicorn Ants
But figured he really understood me when we made it in
Ignaz Wisdom's bathroom.

But next day he sent me a leaf from his Smokey Mountain
retreat

'I love you little Bo-Bo with your delicate golden lions
But there being no Self and No Bars therefore the Zoo of
    your dear Father hath no Lion
You said your mother was mad don't expect me to produce
    the Monster for your Bridegroom.'

Confused dazed and exalted bethought me of real lion
    starved in his stink in Harlem
Opened the door the room was filled with the bomb blast
    of his anger
He roaring hungrily at the plaster walls but nobody could
    hear him outside thru the window
My eye caught the edge of the red neighbor apartment
    building standing in deafening stillness

We gazed at each other his implacable yellow eye in the
    red halo of fur
Waxed rheumy on my own but he stopped roaring and
    bared a fang greeting.
I turned my back and cooked broccoli for supper on an
    iron gas stove
boilt water and took a hot bath in the old tub under the
    sink board.

He didn't eat me, tho I regretted him starving in my
    presence.
Next week he wasted away a sick rug full of bones wheaten
    hair falling out
enraged and reddening eye as he lay aching huge hairy
    head on his paws
by the egg-crate bookcase filled up with thin volumes of
    Plato, & Buddha.
Sat by his side every night averting my eyes from his
    hungry motheaten face

stopped eating myself he got weaker and roared at night
while I had nightmares
Eaten by lion in bookstore on Cosmic Campus, a lion myself starved by Professor Kandisky, dying in a lion's
flophouse circus,
I woke up mornings the lion still added dying on the
floor – 'Terrible Presence!' I cried 'Eat me or die!'

It got up that afternoon – walked to the door with its paw
on the wall to steady its trembling body
Let out a soul rending creak from the bottomless roof of
his mouth
thundering from my floor to heaven heavier than a volcano
at night in Mexico
Pushed the door open and said in a gravelly voice 'Not
this time Baby – but I will be back again.'

Lion that eats my mind now for a decade knowing only
your hunger
Not the bliss of your satisfaction O roar of the Universe
how am I chosen
In this life I have heard your promise I am ready to die I
have served
Your starved and ancient Presence O Lord I wait in my
room at your Mercy.

Magic Psalm

Because this world is on the wing and what cometh no man
can know

O Phantom that my mind pursues from year to year descend
from heaven to this shaking flesh

catch up my fleeting eye in the vast Ray that knows no
bounds – Inseparable – Master –

Giant outside Time with all its falling leaves – Genius of
the Universe – Magician in Nothingness where appear
red clouds –

Unspeakable King of the roads that are gone – Unintel-
ligible Horse riding out of the graveyard – Sunset
spread over Cordillera and insect – Gnarl Moth –

Griever – Laugh with no mouth, Heart that never had
flesh to die – Promise that was not made – Reliever,
whose blood burns in a million animals wounded –

O Mercy, Destroyer of the World, O Mercy, Creator of
Breasted Illusions, O Mercy, cacophanous war-
mouthed doveling, Come,

invade my body with the sex of God, choke up my nostrils
with corruption's infinite caress,

transfigure me to slimy worms of pure sensate transcendency I'm still alive,

croak my voice with uglier than reality, a psychic tomato
speaking Thy million mouths,

Myriad-tongued my Soul, Monster or Angel, Lover that
comes to fuck me forever – white gown on the Eyeless
Squid –

Asshole of the Universe into which I disappear – Elastic
Hand that spoke to Crane – Music that passes into the
phonograph of years from another Millennium – Ear
of the buildings of NY –

That which I believe – have seen – seek endlessly in leaf
  dog eye – fault always, lack – which makes me think –
Desire that created me, Desire I hide in my body, Desire all
  Man know Death, Desire surpassing the Babylonian
  possible world
that makes my flesh shake orgasm of Thy Name which I
  don't know never will never speak –
Speak to Mankind to say the great bell tolls a golden tone on
  iron balconies in every million universe,
I am Thy prophet come home this world to scream an unbearable Name thru my 5 senses hideous sixth
that knows Thy Hand on its invisible phallus, covered with
  electric bulbs of death –
Peace, Resolver where I mess up illusion, Softmouth Vagina
  that enters my brain from above, Ark-Dove with a
  bough of Death.

Drive me crazy, God I'm ready for disintegration of my
  mind, disgrace me in the eye of the earth,
attack my hairy heart with terror eat my cock Invisible
  croak of deathfrog leap on me pack of heavy dogs
  salivating light,
devour my brain One flow of endless consciousness, I'm
  scared of your promise must make scream my prayer
  in fear –
Descend O Light Creator & Eater of Mankind, disrupt the
  world in its madness of bombs and murder,
Volcanos of flesh over London, on Paris a rain of eyes –
  truckloads of angelhearts besmearing Kremlin walls –
  the skullcup of light to New York –
myriad jewelled feet on the terraces of Pekin – veils of
  electrical gas descending over India – cities of Bacteria
  invading the brain – the Soul escaping into the rubber
  waving mouths of Paradise –

This is the Great Call, this is the Tocsin of the Eternal War,
  this is the cry of Mind slain in Nebulae,
this is the Golden Bell of the Church that has never existed,
  this is the Boom in the heart of the sunbeam, this is the
  trumpet of the Worm at Death,
Appeal of the handless castrate grab Alm golden seed of
  Futurity thru the quake & volcan of the world –
Shovel my feet under the Andes, splatter my brains on the
  Sphinx, drape my beard and hair over Empire State
  Building,
cover my belly with hands of moss, fill up my ears with your
  lightning, blind me with prophetic rainbows
That I taste the shit of Being at last, that I touch Thy
  genitals in the palmtree,
that the vast Ray of Futurity enter my mouth to sound Thy
  Creation Forever Unborn, O Beauty invisible to my
  Century!
that my prayer surpass my understanding, that I lay my
  vanity at Thy foot, that I no longer fear Judgement
  over Allen of this world
born in Newark come into Eternity in New York crying
  again in Peru for human Tongue to psalm the Unspeakable,
that I surpass desire for transcendency and enter the calm
  water of the universe
that I ride out this wave, not drown forever in the flood of
  my imagination
that I not be slain thru my own insane magic, this crime be
  punished in merciful jails of Death,
men understand my speech out of their own Turkish heart,
  the prophets aid me with Proclamation,
the Seraphim acclaim Thy Name, Thyself at once in one
  huge Mouth of Universe make meat reply.

MORE ABOUT PENGUINS

Penguin Book News, an attractively illustrated magazine which appears every month, contains details of all the new books issued by Penguins as they are published. Every four months it is supplemented by *Penguins in Print*, which is a complete list of all books published by Penguins which are still available. (There are well over two thousand of these.)

A specimen copy of *Penguin Book News* can be sent to you free on request, and you can become a regular subscriber at 3s. for twelve issues (with the complete lists). Just write to Dept EP, Penguin Books Ltd, Harmondsworth, Middlesex, enclosing a cheque or postal order, and your name will be added to the mailing list.

Some other books published by Penguins are described on the following pages.

Note: *Penguin Book News* and *Penguins in Print*
are not available in the U.S.A. or Canada

YEVTUSHENKO

SELECTED POEMS

Yevgeny Yevtushenko is the fearless spokesman of his generation in Russia. In verse that is young, fresh, and outspoken he frets at restraint and injustice, as in his now famous protest over the Jewish pogrom at Kiev.

But he can write lyrically, too, of the simple things of humanity – love, a birthday, a holiday in Georgia. And in 'Zima Junction' he brilliantly records his impressions on a visit to his home in Siberia.

THE PENGUIN BOOK OF RUSSIAN VERSE

EDITED BY DIMITRI OBOLENSKY

The belief, current in the West, that Russian poetry has its beginnings in the early nineteenth century is, though misguided, understandable. The unexampled blossoming of this poetry between 1810 and 1830, in a newly developed language easily recognizable as modern Russian and in a literary context avowedly European, makes the age of Pushkin seem like a sudden flowering in a wilderness. Eighteenth-century Russian literature, without which Pushkin himself cannot be properly understood, is in the West largely unknown or dismissed as derivative and 'pseudo-classical'; while further back, the Russian Middle Ages extend in an ill-defined penumbra, out of which inexplicably emerge a number of heroic poems transmitted by word of mouth from generation to generation, some of which have been translated into languages of Western Europe.

This collection of Russian verse, which extends from heroic poems of the twelfth century to the work of poets still living, is accompanied by plain prose translations and an excellent introduction.

SELECTED PROSE

T. S. ELIOT

This Peregrine selection from his prose writings is designed to demonstrate the range and penetration of T. S. Eliot's criticism. Edited and introduced, with his approval, by Mr John Hayward, it provides a comprehensive introduction to one of the finest and most original critical minds of our time. The twelve essays and addresses printed here in full, and the selected passages from some forty others, fall into two groups. The first consists of literary criticism, chosen from Mr Eliot's continuous work in this field over the past forty-five years, with particular emphasis on poetry and individual poets. The second group comprises his mature opinions on the human situation in general, and more especially his views on religion, culture, and education in contemporary life. The fact that some of the material in both groups is not readily accessible will increase the interest and value of this selection as a work of reference to a critic who has exercised a profound and exciting influence on the thought and sensibility of the age.

A CRITICAL HISTORY OF ENGLISH POETRY

HERBERT GRIERSON AND J. C. SMITH

This famous work was the result of the wartime collaboration of two Scottish scholars. Their tracing of the course of English poetry has been described by *The Times Literary Supplement* as a 'volume of masterly compression'. They deliberately spend most time on the greatest poets, believing that, significant as traditions and influences are, the great poet himself affects the spirit of his age and moulds the tradition he has inherited. At the same time, enough attention is paid to minor poets to make the book historically complete, and to fill in the most important links in the chain of poetic development. Thus Gower is here, as well as Chaucer; Patmore, as well as Browning. Both in scope and in detail *A Critical History of English Poetry* is a distinguished and valuable work.

'Alive with witty and just appreciation of the best that has been done in our tongue' – *Scotsman*

THE PENGUIN POETS

SOME VOLUMES BY INDIVIDUAL POETS

ROBERT GRAVES *
selected by himself

HÖLDERLIN
edited by Michael Hamburger

D. H. LAWRENCE *
selected poems

LORCA
edited by J. L. Gili

W. H. AUDEN †
selected by himself

HILAIRE BELLOC *
collected verse

JOHN DONNE
edited by John Hayward

WILLIAM BLAKE
edited by J. Bronowski

E. E. CUMMINGS †
selected poems

*NOT FOR SALE IN THE U.S.A.
†NOT FOR SALE IN THE U.S.A. OR CANADA

THE PENGUIN POETS

SOME ANTHOLOGIES

THE PENGUIN BOOK OF GERMAN VERSE
introduced and edited by Leonard Forster

THE PENGUIN BOOK OF ENGLISH VERSE
edited by John Hayward

THE PENGUIN BOOK OF CONTEMPORARY VERSE*
edited by Kenneth Allott

THE PENGUIN BOOK OF CHINESE VERSE
introduced and edited by A. R. Davis

THE PENGUIN BOOK OF ANIMAL VERSE*
introduced and edited by George MacBeth

THE PENGUIN BOOK OF JAPANESE VERSE
*translated and with an introduction by Geoffrey Bownas
and Anthony Thwaite*

*NOT FOR SALE IN THE U.S.A.

THE NEW POETRY

Selected and introduced by A. Alvarez

'This is a personal anthology. It makes no claims to give a sample of every kind of verse now being written in Great Britain. I am, however, trying to represent what I think is the most significant work of the British poets who began to come into their own in the fifties. I have also included the work of four American writers who, although established before then, seem, as I try to explain in the Introduction, to be concerned with problems that some of the new generation of poets over here are beginning to face.

'This is not, in short, an anthology for the reader who wants a complete guide to the contemporary poetic scene; but then, anyone who wants that already has a large number of excellent collections from which to choose. In this book I am, instead, simply attempting to give my idea of what, that really matters, has happened to poetry in England during the last decade' – A. Alvarez

BAUDELAIRE

Edited by Francis Scarfe

A poet whose work is so complex and diverse, though apparently so simple and unified, as Baudelaire's is not to be summarized in any convenient formula. Yet many attempts of this kind have been made; they are useful and have to be taken seriously. A modern Dante? This suggestion, first made in 1857 by Thierry, has been discussed and modified by T. S. Eliot who would be more satisfied with a comparison with Goethe. 'The Swift of poetry,' suggested Lytton Strachey: but they meet only in their disgust, wit, and gloom, and Baudelaire is the bigger of the two. Aldous Huxley called him 'a bored satanist' and Lionel Johnson stated: 'Baudelaire sings sermons.' He has been described as 'the tragic sophist', as 'too Christian', and as a 'Near-Jansenist'.

In this selection Francis Scarfe has placed the poems, for the first time, in a roughly chronological order while trying to preserve the 'cycles' into which they fall. A plain prose translation is appended to each poem.

PENGUIN MODERN POETS

This series is an attempt to introduce contemporary poetry to the general reader by publishing some thirty poems by each of three modern poets in a single volume. In each case the selection will be made to illustrate the poet's characteristics in style and form. Further volumes are in preparation.